DISCUS
Breeding for Beginners
Jack Wattley

A Little Discus History

Has the so-called "discus craze" hit American shores? Absolutely! Discusfishes, genus *Symphysodon*, made their first popularity push in Europe in the 1960s. At that time, the majority of discus being exported from Brazil and Colombia were being sold in Europe, where the exporters could command a much higher price than in the United States. The brown discus, *Symphysodon aequifasciata axelrodi*, had already made its appearance here in America, while at the same time in Europe importers were acquiring *Symphysodon aequifasciata haraldi*, the blue discus, as well as *Symphysodon discus*, the Heckel discus. Thereafter, the green discus, *Symphysodon aequifasciata aequifasciata*, was found near Tefe in the state of Amazonas, Brazil and made its way to the USA and Europe about the same time.

Where do discus come from? Most discus are found in Brazil and in eastern Colombia, with small numbers occasionally found in streams in Guyana, Suriname, and Venezuela. In the collecting areas where discus are found, the water is cloudy (turbid) and is referred to as "white water." One finds *Symphysodon discus* in the small tributaries of the Rio Negro. *Symphysodon aequifasciata aequifasciata* (the green dis-

© T.F.H. Publications, Inc.

Distributed in the UNITED STATES to the Pet Trade by T.F.H. Publications, Inc., 1 TFH Plaza, Neptune City, NJ 07753; on the Internet at www.tfh.com; in CANADA by Rolf C. Hagen Inc., 3225 Sartelon St., Montreal, Quebec H4R 1E8; Pet Trade by H & L Pet Supplies Inc., 27 Kingston Crescent, Kitchener, Ontario N2B 2T6; in ENGLAND by T.F.H. Publications, PO Box 74, Havant PO9 5TT; in AUSTRALIA AND THE SOUTH PACIFIC by T.F.H. (Australia), Pty. Ltd., Box 149, Brookvale 2100 N.S.W., Australia; in NEW ZEALAND by Brooklands Aquarium Ltd., 5 McGiven Drive, New Plymouth, RD1 New Zealand; in SOUTH AFRICA by Rolf C. Hagen S.A. (PTY.) LTD., P.O. Box 201199, Durban North 4016, South Africa; in JAPAN by T.F.H. Publications. Published by T.F.H. Publications, Inc.

MANUFACTURED IN THE
UNITED STATES OF AMERICA
BY T.F.H. PUBLICATIONS, INC.

A LITTLE DISCUS HISTORY

Harald Schultz, for whom the discus *Symphysodon aequifasciata haraldi* was named.

Colombia and Brazil. Many aquarists refer to the green discus as either the Peruvian green or the Tefe green. After having personally collected discus along the Colombian-Peruvian border (the Putamayo River), as well as in Brazil near Lake Tefe and Fonte Boa, I can say that the Peruvian discus and the Tefe discus are in my opinion one and the same.

Traveling east along the Amazon River, past Coari, one encounters the blue discus, *Symphysodon aequifasciata haraldi*, named after Harald Schultz. The Rio Purus is home to the blue discus. East of Manaus, the brown discus, *Symphysodon aequifasciata axelrodi*, can be found. In this general vicinity are also *Symphysodon discus willischwartzi* and the brown/red Alenquer discus.

Once we move past the species and subspecies of the wild discus and into the different varieties of tank-bred discus, the colors and names are countless. (As a matter of fact, there is plenty of confusion and controversy about the names of species and subspecies of wild discus as well, but let's not get into that.) At the time of my first discus-collecting venture in Brazil, Willi Schwartz in Manaus was marketing his top-of-the-line wild-caught blue discus as a "royal blue" discus. These fish, with their superior color, brought a much higher price than the normal-colored blue discus and were sold initially in Europe.

Willi Schwartz, who, with Axelrod and Schultz, opened up the Amazon for discus collecting. Photo by Dr. Herbert R. Axelrod.

In 1963 I was able to collect a small number of attractive blue discus and several years later crossed these fish with green discus that I had collected in a tributary of the Rio Jurua in Brazil. What color do you get when mixing blue and green? Turquoise, of course! We thus marketed the offspring of this crossing as the Jack Wattley Turquoise discus. Since that time, tank-raised discus have appeared on the scene with such names as Red Ruby, Blue Sapphire, Princess Ruby, Gold Rainbow, and Pearl Red, and the list could go on and on.

In the 1970s, interest in discus waned a bit in Europe, resuming in full force in the early 1980s, at which time I introduced my Jack Wattley Turquoise discus to the hobby in Japan. The Japanese, however, were not quite ready for discus at that time. By 1984, interest in discus in Japan and the United States had begun to skyrocket, and at present the key word in freshwater tropical fish is discus.

Without question, the greatest contribution concerning a new color variety has been the development in Thailand of the Pigeon Blood discus. This fish has been crossed with other discus, resulting in a large number of exciting new

Dr. Herbert R. Axelrod, for whom the Brown Discus, *Symphysodon aequifasciata axelrodi*, was named. Photo by Evelyn Axelrod.

color forms. The Pigeon Blood discus has been sold throughout the world, and it would be difficult to find a discus hobbyist who does not have a few Pigeon Bloods or has not heard of the strain.

Contents

Now that we have had a little history lesson about our favorite cichlid, the discus, we will discuss one of the most frequently asked questions about discus: are discus fish easy to maintain? The answer is "yes" if some very simple guidelines are followed. Unfortunately, however, some years ago the assumption was made that discus were difficult to keep, and for a long time selectively manipulated facts were perpetuated to support this assumption. In following sections we'll go step by step through the entire procedure of successfully keeping discus in a manner that will be easy for the first-time discus aquarist to understand. One of our goals will be to provide new discus owners with enough information not only to allow them to just keep discus alive but also to attempt to breed them.

Aquarium Equipment and Furnishings 22

The Right Water for Discus 5

Tankmates for Discus ... 29

Purchasing Discus .. 43

Feeding Discus... 34

Breeding 47

Diseases 62

THE RIGHT WATER FOR DISCUS

The Pigeon Blood Discus is a tank-developed strain not found in Nature. It appears under many other common names depending upon the source, but it was originally developed by Gan Aquarium Fish Farm in Singapore. Photo by K.L.Chew.

The Right Water For Discus

The first-time discus hobbyist need not immerse himself in the study of water chemistry. At many of the discus seminars where I have given presentations, I have seen potential discus enthusiasts frightened away from the hobby after listening to a speaker go into minute detail concerning water chemistry. Successful discus keeping is not the purely scientific endeavor that many people want you to believe. We personally monitor at least twenty telephone calls or faxes per day concerning discus, many coming from people informing us of their success with discus using nothing but the local tap water. Others tell us of their use of either reverse osmosis or deionization for treating their water when in fact neither one of those processes would be necessary in their locality.

Let us assume that you will be using city water or, if necessary, reverse osmosis water. You have already purchased the necessary water test kits for pH and water hardness, a kit to measure the chlorine and chloramine content of the water, and an ammonia/nitrite/nitrate kit. These water testing kits can be purchased in your local aquarium shop at minimal cost.

The pH kit you have purchased will most likely be the type using either a liquid reagent or paper probes in the form of disposable strips. The paper probes are very efficient and quick reading, whereas the test kits using the liquid reagent take more time for a reading but are generally a bit more accurate. The liquid reagent to measure the pH from a range of 4.5 to 7.5— certainly in the range of all deionized water— is bromothymol blue. There are many other pH testing kits available that are more expensive, but for the beginning discus hobbyist, as well as for most other aquarists, the above-mentioned inexpensive pH

The city of Tefe on Lago Tefe which is part of Rio Tefe. One hundred years ago it was an important rubber center. It is now nothing more than a ghost of its original splendor. Photo by Dr. Herbert R. Axelrod.

The Tefe Discus, *Symphysodon aequifasciata aequifasciata.* **Photographed and collected by Dr. Herbert R. Axelrod. This is a wild-caught fish.**

THE RIGHT WATER FOR DISCUS

kits will yield satisfactory results. A very successful California-based discus breeder who houses his fish in a state-of-the-art hatchery uses the bromothymol blue reagent for all his pH readings.

What pH do we want to maintain in our discus tanks? Most discus keepers,

Fishes that come from soft, acid waters can benefit from buffering against the water's mineral content which causes water hardness. Some preparations contain vitamins and beneficial bacteria. Photo courtesy of Tropical Science.

hobbyists and commercial breeders alike, maintain a pH of 6.0 to 6.5, both readings being on the acid side (with pH 7.0 being neutral and anything above 7.0 being alkaline). But I have seen Southeast Asian discus breeders successfully raise their fish in 7.0 to 7.4 pH waters. If your pH absolutely must be lowered, however, there are several methods of doing so. If you have soft water with no buffering capacity, the pH can easily be lowered effectively by the use of high quality peat. Not only will peat lower the pH in soft water, but it will also remove some carbonate hardness. On the other hand, if the water to be treated is hard with a high conductivity, the peat will accomplish virtually nothing. Unknown to many tropical fish hobbyists is that peat in the aquarium has a very short life span, depending, of course, on the amount of water circulating through it. Most hobbyists using peat leave it in the aquarium much too long, with all the acid-producing properties long since leached out into the aquarium water.

How is the peat to be placed into the tank? It must be dampened first, then placed in a fine mesh bag to prevent dispersal throughout the tank, and finally positioned in a filter box so that the water can pass through it. Be certain that your peat does not contain any fertilizers, bark, or other harmful additions. It must be pure peat. With your pH test kit you can determine how long the peat is effective. For example, if you have been able to reduce the pH from 7.5 to 6.5 by using the peat for several days, and the pH is stabilized at 6.5 and not dropping any lower, you can be certain that the peat has exhausted all its acid properties. What if the pH has dropped below 6.5 or even below 6.0? We have had situations where the pH has

The Green Discus from Tefe. The discus in that area differ depending upon whether they come from Lake (Lago) Tefe or Rio (River) Tefe. Photo of a wild specimen by Fumitoshi Mori.

THE RIGHT WATER FOR DISCUS

The Brown Discus, *Symphysodon aequifasciata axelrodi*, coming from eastern Brazil from Belem to Santarem along the Amazon. Photo by Arend van den Nieuwenhuizen.

THE RIGHT WATER FOR DISCUS

To have the most brilliantly colored, healthy discus, you need clean water, a proper diet and natural extracts from the kinds of plants and soil found in the fish's natural habitat. Fortunately the latter can be obtained from carefully prepared additives that are safe for all fishes including discus and killifish fry. Photo courtesy of Aquarium Pharmaceuticals, Inc.

Discus in their Amazonian streams spend their entire lives in soft, acid water that, at times, could almost be classified as distilled water. Is it necessary to duplicate those Amazonian conditions in our aquariums? Not at all! Water hardness is important, but not as important as some discus aquarists would have you believe. We continually hear of successful discus spawnings in water with a total dissolved solids (ppm) reading as high as 400, and we know of one breeder raising discus in water of 700 ppm! Soft water will generally read from 1 ppm to more or less 70 ppm, and water with a 100 ppm to 125 ppm reading would be considered medium soft.

Inexpensive water hardness kits are available in all good aquarium shops. You can also determine very quickly whether the local tap water is soft or hard by washing your hands with

dropped to as low as 5.0. Is that bad? Not really. A pH reading of approximately 5.0 to 5.5 is like having an insurance policy in your discus aquarium, for two reasons. For one, most *Pseudomonas* and *Aeromonas* bacteria cannot thrive in such a low pH; for the other, if there are traces of ammonia in the aquarium, it will be in the form of ammonium, which is basically less harmful to fishes than the form of ammonia that exists in alkaline water.

If your municipal water is medium-hard to hard with a high pH, the pH will not be lowered by the use of peat. In that case it will be necessary to use phosphoric acid, hydrochloric acid, or buffering agents that can be obtained in an aquarium shop. Obviously you're going to be better off if you can use the buffering agents and avoid getting involved with dangerous acids.

Brown Discus, *Symphysodon aequifasciata axelrodi,* from Santarem, Brazil. Photo by Dr. Herbert R. Axelrod.

THE RIGHT WATER FOR DISCUS

Jack Wattley, the author of this book, developed what he calls the *Wattley Coerulea*. This is a very expensive color variety. Photo by Fumitoshi Mori.

THE RIGHT WATER FOR DISCUS

The Brown Discus, *Symphysodon aequifasciata axelrodi*, from the Rio Xingu near Porto de Maz. Photo by Dr. Herbert R. Axelrod.

THE RIGHT WATER FOR DISCUS

soap and water. If the water is hard with many mineral salts it will be difficult to get a good soap lather, whereas soft water with soap will produce a good lather.

REVERSE OSMOSIS WATER

Reverse osmosis water, or R.O. water, is water that has passed through a membrane under pressure, removing up to 98% of bacteria, viruses, mineral salts, and heavy metals and thus becoming very much like distilled water. Reverse osmosis for discus keeping was first introduced in the USA and in Canada, and later put into use in Europe. Today reverse osmosis water is used throughout the world for advanced discus keeping.

To attain your desired hardness (ppm) when using reverse osmosis water, it is necessary to blend this water with either your local municipal water or well water, or else to add trace elements to the reverse osmosis water. Neither discus nor any other fish can live in reverse osmosis water without adding at least some minerals back into the water. A detailed account of reverse osmosis can be found in my book *Discus for the Perfectionist*.

We frequently hear from hobbyists inquiring about reverse osmosis who have just one or two breeding pairs of discus. Our recommendation

The Blue Discus, *Symphysodon aequifasciata haraldi*. This was the type specimen collected by Dr. Axelrod in the Rio Purus. Photo by Dr. Herbert R. Axelrod. Inset: A view of the port of the city of Tapaua, Rio Purus, Brazil, the home of the Blue Discus. Photo by Dr. Herbert R. Axelrod.

to them, if they do indeed require artificial water, is to purchase distilled water from a supermarket. If their one or two breeding tanks are like ours in size (20 gallons), it would probably be more economical to buy distilled water and combine it with the city water when making water changes. Needless to say, the amount of city water needed to combine with your reverse osmosis water, in order to reach the desired ppm hardness, depends on the hardness of the city or well water. A hobbyist in Texas, for example, where water generally is hard, would use less city water than someone in New England, where water generally is soft.

CHLORINE AND CHLORAMINES IN MUNICIPAL WATER

Either chlorine alone or chloramine (a combination of chlorine and ammonia) is added to most city water for the control of bacteria. Do we remove them? If we have chloramines in our water, it is essential to remove them before using the water for discus keeping. All good aquarium shops in areas where chloramines are added to the city water have water conditioners for their removal. In our discus hatchery, we remove chloramines by passing the water through activated carbon. If your method of chloramine removal is using activated carbon, then it is extremely important to be certain that the carbon is still good, i.e., active. Chlorine can also be removed by activated carbon, as well as by heavy aeration, or by the addition of sodium thiosulphate, which will neutralize the chlorine. In many instances the removal of chlorine is not necessary. If your water changes are minimal and the chlorine content of the city water is minimal, it will not be necessary to be concerned about chlorine removal.

Lastly, we come to the kit for measuring the ammonia (NH_3), nitrite (NO_2), and nitrate (NO_3). Keep in mind that there are other water quality measuring kits available, such as those for measuring oxygen content

A wild-caught specimen of the Heckel Discus, *Symphysodon discus discus*, which was collected and photographed by Dr. Axelrod in the Rio Negro, Brazil.

THE RIGHT WATER FOR DISCUS

The tank-made blue discus also known as the Shirase Royal Thunder Flash, Tarzoo Blue, Mack Powder Blue, Blue Turquoise, etc. Photo by Fumitoshi Mori.

The so-called Shirase Red Thunder Flash, a name given to this tank-made discus color variety. Photo by Fumitoshi Mori.

THE RIGHT WATER FOR DISCUS

The Blue-head Discus Heckel collected and photographed by Dr. Herbert R. Axelrod from the Rio Jau, a tributary of the Rio Negro near Moura, Brazil.

of the water and those for determining iron content, etc., but these kits in most cases will not be necessary. Your ammonia/nitrite/nitrate kit, with regular use, will immediately tell you whether the water in your aquarium is suitable.

Ammonia and nitrite, and to a lesser extent nitrate, have no place in the discus aquarium or in any other aquarium. Their appearance in the aquarium can usually be traced to poor water quality, inferior filtration, overfeeding, or overcrowding the aquarium - or, in extreme cases, a combination of all these conditions!

Minute levels of ammonia and nitrite are constantly being released into the aquarium by the fish, in the form of uneaten food, fecal matter, and urine. Discus should not have to tolerate levels of ammonia or nitrite higher than 25 ppm. In the successful aquarium, the beneficial nitrifying bacteria will convert the toxic ammonia to nitrite, and then to nitrate, which is relatively benign. If the pH of the aquarium water is lower than 6.3 - 6.4, the potentially harmful ammonia will have been converted to the much less damaging ammonium (NH_3), although in some aquarium waters both ammonia and ammonium can be present. Even low levels of ammonia and nitrite can be the cause of disease outbreaks, due to the continual stress that the fish must live with.

Regular water changes, proper filtration, and an intelligent feeding program will keep the ammonia and nitrite at an acceptable level. We employ an "overkill" method of control by making daily water changes of approximately 40%. An added bonus of making 40% water changes is the fact that the young discus grow at an accelerated rate. The discus hobbyist can get by nicely with two 25% water changes weekly and a pH of 6.5.

FILTRATION AND WATER CHANGES

Filtration for the first-time discus hobbyist can be very simple, so we will not complicate matters by describing intricate filtration systems used by some fanciers who aim to make discus keeping a scientific endeavor, which it need not be! Box filters, both inside and outside, are not in reality biological filters, but they are

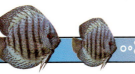

THE RIGHT WATER FOR DISCUS

efficient in removing uneaten food, fecal matter, and other solids from the aquarium. The filter materials generally used are activated carbon and a filter floss. In purchasing the carbon, make certain that it is labeled "activated carbon" and not charcoal. There is a big difference between the two, with the charcoal being virtually useless, as its lifespan is very short.

The floss material can be nylon or dacron and can be purchased cut to size to fit on top of the carbon bed in the filter box. As the floss material becomes clogged with uneaten foods and other solids, it can be quickly removed from the filter, cleaned in fresh water, and replaced.

External canister-style power filters can make use of a number of different filter media in varying combinations to obtain maximum efficiency. Photo courtesy of Renaissance International, Inc.

The Wattley Coerulea developed further in Japan. Photo by Fumitoshi Mori. The Wattley varieties have formed the basis of many present-day color varieties of discus.

THE RIGHT WATER FOR DISCUS

The Jack Wattley Scribbled Discus strain. Photo by Fumitoshi Mori.

A tank-raised Brown Discus, *Symphysodon aequifasciata axelrodi*. Photo by Fumitoshi Mori.

THE RIGHT WATER FOR DISCUS

A wild-caught Green Discus from Tefe. The diet change probably caused the loss of yellow (yellow+blue = green) in this specimen. Photo by Fumitoshi Mori.

Commercial discus breeders often take the simplest route by using nothing but sponge filters that stand approximately one inch off the bottom of the tank. These are very efficient and time-saving. They can act effectively as biological filters if they are of sufficient size and if the flow of water moving through them is sufficient to maintain a good thriving colony of beneficial (aerobic) bacteria. These sponge filters must be cleaned out in fresh water; the frequency depends upon many factors, such as how many fish are in the aquarium and the frequency and volume of water changes and feedings.

Many of the canister filters and power filters use zeolite, which, if used properly, can control ammonia build-up in the tank. The claim has often been made that the zeolite bed acts as an area for aerobic cultivation, but generally the zeolite has to be replaced by the time the aerobic bacteria are becoming established. Wet/dry trickle filtration has become very sophisticated and is currently used by many discus hobbyists.

Most Southeast Asian discus hobbyists and commercial breeders omit filtration in any form, claiming that frequent water changes preclude the need for any form of filtration. I would have to state that I agree with them as long as the water changes are, indeed, frequent, with at least four weekly water changes made of approximately 30% each time. Naturally, if the aquarium is overcrowded or if you have embarked on a heavy feeding program to promote quick growth in the fish, the water changes should be increased to once or twice daily. If your priorities are such that you can't or do not want to make these frequent water changes, you will have to resort to filtration.

Making water changes necessitates having a holding facility of some sort to house the new water to be used. The size of the facility depends on the number of gallons of water to be used. If, for example, you have two aquariums of 50 gallons each and you are going to remove approximately 17 gallons from each tank, you should have a

THE RIGHT WATER FOR DISCUS

The river strain of the Tefe Discus, *Symphysodon a. aequifasciata*. Photo by Hans J. Mayland.

holding tank of at least 35 to 40 gallons. In this holding facility, the new water can be heated to the proper aquarium temperature, and the chlorine or chloramines can be removed. There are areas in the United States where the chlorine content of the water is so low that it poses no danger to the fish, in which case the water can be used almost immediately. Nevertheless, the temperature and the pH must be adjusted to some degree before adding the new water to your tank.

It is not at all necessary to make an exact adjustment for the temperature or for the pH. If you maintain a water temperature of 84 degrees Fahrenheit in your discus tank(s) and the incoming water has a temperature of 80 degrees Fahrenheit (with a 30% water change), the slight temporary decrease in temperature will present no problem. The same situation exists regarding a light pH change in the incoming water, as long as the incoming water has a slightly higher pH. Let us assume that your aquarium water has a pH of 6.4 and the new water reads pH 6.7 or 6.8. This is acceptable. Needless to say, if your aquarium water pH is 6.4 and the new water reads 6.9 - 7.0 or above, then an adjustment must be made.

With all our adult fish, including those that are not breeding, we try to make a 40% water change daily. There are times when we are not able to make the daily water change, although in our hatchery this is a priority. For young discus we make a 50% water change daily. (A young discus is any fish that is still in its growing stage, a period of approximately eleven to fourteen months.) If you want to see incredible growth on young discus, or on any other fish for that matter, make a 95% water change daily! In doing this you must monitor both the pH and the water temperature closely. A small variance with a 30% water change in most cases is not significant, but a 95% water change requires a much closer look.

This fish was offered for sale by the World Wide Fish Farm, Hong Kong as a *strain of wild discus*, whatever that means. But, according to Dr. Axelrod, no such discus appears in the wild. Photo by Lo Wing Yat.

Aquarium Equipment and Furnishings

Aquarium heaters are necessary unless one lives in a region where the outside temperature never drops below 80 degrees Fahrenheit. It is essential to purchase the finest quality heater you possibly can. Heaters can malfunction, with the result being perhaps the total loss of the discus habitat in the tank. A discus breeder I know dates all his heaters and after a year discards them, replacing the year-old heaters with new heaters. In that way he probably has as much assurance as possible that his heaters will function properly.

Submersible heaters of good quality are popular in discus tanks. Depending on the size of the aquarium, a second heater can certainly act as an "insurance policy" in the tank should the first heater malfunction in any way. It would be prudent to use two heaters in the typical 55-gallon tanks that are very popular for keeping discus. We do not use aquarium heaters for our discus, as our hatchery is heated when necessary by propane gas, but a good rule-of-thumb indicator of how much wattage is needed in the aquarium is to figure that approximately five watts per gallon will more than maintain the proper water temperature. Thermometers and heaters go hand in hand, so a high-quality thermometer is another essential piece of equipment.

When installing lighting for the discus tank the hobbyist

The Willi Schwartz Discus, *Symphysodon discus willischwartzi*, discovered and photographed by Dr. Herbert R. Axelrod in the Rio Abacaxis, a northern tributary of the Rio Madeira.

AQUARIUM EQUIPMENT AND FURNISHINGS

can go in one of two directions. I have yet to see a commercial discus breeder using artificial lighting over each tank, and in nearly all cases neither the commercial hatchery nor the individual tanks are aesthetically pleasing. The discus hobbyist, however, not being commercially motivated in any way, can very easily create a beautiful discus habitat by employing the proper lighting, discus hobbyist uses depends entirely on what he desires to accomplish. If the plants are to be given the same priority as the discus, and if the tank is deep and of a large size, it might be best to use metal halide lamps. Although they are more expensive than the normal fluorescent lights, the additional cost of the lamps would be offset by the fact that no aquarium reflector would be required, as the

Many of the lights that are especially designed for reef tanks can be adapted for use in discus aquariums, with some to promote plant growth and others designed to bring out the color of the fish. Aquarium reflectors can serve a dual purpose, because we all know that discus are great jumpers, and a full-hood reflector can prevent the unnecessary loss of a favorite fish.

This perfect discus aquarium features many wide-leafed plants, lots of hiding places, yet open water in which the discus can swim. Photo by Bernd Degen.

plants, and, of course, the discus themselves.

In the aquarium trade incandescent lighting has been, for the most part, discarded in favor of fluorescent lighting, which is less expensive to use and does not generate any unwanted heat directly over the aquarium. The type of lighting that the halide lamps are suspended directly over the tank. Because they do generate a fair amount of heat, they must hang some distance above the tank.

Fluorescent lights in combination with reflectors are commonly used by hobbyists in most discus aquariums utilizing cool white lights.

AQUATIC PLANTS IN THE DISCUS AQUARIUM

Most aquarists agree that live aquarium plants add to the aesthetic appearance of the aquarium, but keep in mind that although some plants do quite well in discus tanks, some do very poorly. The ones I'm covering here are among those that do well, but

Discus of any color variety can be kept together providing there is plenty of hiding places in dense vegetation.

of course the coverage is not exhaustive.

Ceratopteris thalictroides, better known as water sprite, can be planted, although we feel it is much more suitable in the discus tank as a floating plant. With a reflector light over the aquarium, the water sprite will settle in

Ceratopteris, water sprite, when it is allowed to float. Photo by W. Tomey.

Water sprite when it is planted. Photo by Andre Roth.

quickly and will soon cover the entire surface area of the aquarium. Over time water sprite may necessitate "thinning out" because it grows quickly. Water sprite is a beautiful aquatic plant, and being hardy, it is adaptable to most water conditions.

Other suitable aquatic additions that can be planted in the discus aquarium are the various Amazon swordplants (genus *Echinodorus*). There are several species and varieties generally available that can be planted in the substrate or grown in individual pots. Some of them grow to a large size and can be very impressive-looking in the discus tank. One of the most beautiful discus aquariums I have ever seen was in Germany, where the aquarist had several extra-large Amazon swordplants in ceramic vases. The 100-gallon all-glass tank was bare on the bottom and, in addition to six large discus, included a fine piece of driftwood.

Discus examining an Amazon swordplant, *Echinodorus*, upon which they will deposit their eggs. Photo by Bernd Degen.

Driftwood can certainly be used in a discus aquarium, but only after it has been properly cured or treated. Many times an aquarium shopkeeper will sell a piece of driftwood from one of his own tanks, in which case one can be reasonably certain that the piece will be safe to use. It is important that the driftwood have no sharp edges that can injure the discus. At times when discus are startled, for whatever reason, they can dash across the tank, and a piece of driftwood or a rock with sharp edges could result in an ugly, damaging wound on the fish. When young discus reach adulthood, they are very much attracted to driftwood as a spawning site. One of the respondents in my book *Discus for the Perfectionist* had a successful spawning of Heckel discus in a large aquarium, where the eggs had been deposited on a piece of driftwood.

AQUARIUM EQUIPMENT AND FURNISHINGS

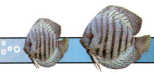

Massive chunks of driftwood in a huge discus tank can be very effective. It even tinges the water a light red. Photo by Bernd Degen.

A scourge in the freshwater irrigation waterways of Florida, *Hygrophila* does very well in discus aquariums. With sufficient light from the outside as well as from the aquarium, *Hygrophila* makes an excellent discus "tankmate." With a reflector light over the aquarium, the plant will quickly grow to the top of the tank where, if necessary, it can easily be trimmed back.

**Hygrophila* suits discus very well. This is the green-white variety. Photo by B. Gregor.*

AQUARIUM EQUIPMENT AND FURNISHINGS

Keeping discus together with larger fishes is a tricky business. Certainly the discus would lose the battle if they fought over a meal! Photo by Bernd Degen.

Tankmates For Discus

One of the first questions that we are asked by hobbyists starting out with their first discus tank is what other fish can be kept with their discus. One must keep in mind that discusfishes are not community tank candidates. Nevertheless, many hobbyists do keep their discus in tanks with other types of tropicals that in most cases are not at all compatible with discus.

What fish can be maintained successfully with discus? I would limit any tankmate selection to the following fishes: *Corydoras* of just about any species, *Paracheirodon axelrodi* (cardinal tetra), *Petitella georgiae* (rummy nose tetra), and *Microgeophagus ramirezi* (ram). All four of these fishes have the same general water requirements as discus have and for the most part come from the same general Amazonian areas where discus are found. I know of several discus hobbyists who have kept rams with their discus and have had both species spawn successfully in the same aquarium.

One interesting point concerning the rummy nose tetra is that the color of its head is an accurate indicator of the quality of the water it's in. In typical discus water the rummy nose tetra, will show a beautiful rose-colored head. But if the water quality is inferior (for the discus as well as for the tetra), the rummy nose's head will be a light gray in color.

Cardinal tetras, *Paracheirodon axelrodi*, have always been suitable companions for discus. They even co-exist in nature. Photo by R. Wederich.

TANKMATES FOR DISCUS

TANKMATES FOR DISCUS

The brilliant Japanese aquarist, photographer and aquarium philosopher, Takashi Amano, designed and decorated this magnificent aquarium just for discus and peaceful small tetras such as *Petitella georgiae*. He called this the GRACE aquarium. Amano wrote a set of three books with magnificent color photos of aquarium arrangements. You simpy MUST see these books. They are called *NATURE AQUARIUM WORLD*.

Discus and angelfish, like this *Pterophyllum altum*, are not good tankmates. The Angelfish carry parasites which may infect discus. Photo by Hans Joachim Richter.

The rummy-nosed tetra, *Petitella georgiae*, is often utilized as a companion of discus. Photo by Hans Joachim Richter.

Several tropicals that definitely should not share aquarium space with discus are occasionally housed with them. Most tetras, for example, have a tendency to bother discus by nipping at their fins or swimming around them in an agitating manner. The cardinal tetra, however, is very placid, as is the rummy nose tetra. Most barbs are extremely nervous fish and have no place in the discus aquarium. Most of the *Botia* species, of which *Botia macracantha*, the clown loach, is a prime example, do not belong in the discus aquarium either. Discus are diurnal and clown loaches are nocturnal, so when your discus are attempting to rest at night, the loaches will be swimming happily throughout the tank disturbing them.

If cardinal tetras are suitable in the discus tank, then why not neon tetras? From the perspective of the discus there certainly would be no problem, but the neon tetra (*Paracheirodon innesi*) comes from cooler waters and fares better in water temperatures of 72 - 75 degrees Fahrenheit. And what about algae-eating *Plecostomus* in the discus tank? Many discus keepers persist in maintaining their discus with Plecos. This is an extremely bad choice, because Plecos, like loaches, are nocturnal, and under the right conditions they will soon outgrow the tank as well.

Angelfish (*Pterophyllum*) are commonly seen with discus in the same tank. Why are these not a good choice? Here's why: angelfish, in many cases, carry intestinal parasites that are easily transmittable to discus kept in the same tank.

TANKMATES FOR DISCUS

There are many kinds of sucker-mouthed catfishes which are generally referred to as *Plecostomus*. This is one of them. They are not recommended for the discus aquarium. Photo by Hans Joachim Richter.

Botia macracantha the clown loach, does not belong in the same tank with discus. Photo by Hans Joachim Richter.

Cardinal tetras are the ideal for the discus tank. Photo by Hans Joachim Richter.

Neon tetras are not suitable for the discus tank because they do not tolerate water in the 80°F. area. Photo by Dr. Herbert R. Axelrod.

The small catfishes of the genus *Corydoras* make excellent additions to the discus tank. This is *Corydoras trilineata*. Photo by Aaron Norman.

The Ram is excellent for the discus tank. They are cichlids, too. Photo by MP&C Piednoir.

Feeding Discus

LIVE FOODS

Discussing the most suitable foods for discus is like opening up the proverbial can of worms. One can talk to a number of successful discus breeders regarding food for discus and hear a number of different views. I will discuss in some detail what we have fed our own discus in the past and what we are currently feeding them. This applies to our growing young fish as well as to our adult fish.

Some years ago the food of choice for discus was live *Tubifex* worms. Not any more! At that time, most of the discus available to hobbyists were wild-caught fish; when fed, they immediately accepted the worms with relish. In their native streams, the discus diet consists largely of the larvae of insects, many of which are worm-like in appearance, so live *Tubifex* worms seemed like a logical substitute. The problem is that nearly all tubificid worms carry internal parasites that can be damaging to discus.

With *Tubifex* out of the running, what other live foods are safe and readily available for discus? Some discus breeders insist that live foods are necessary, so I will discuss (even though I generally don't use them) three foods that are completely safe. The first is *Artemia* (brine shrimp). Newly hatched *Artemia* as a second food for baby discus is used by many breeders, but we try to avoid it because *Artemia* nauplii can harbor

White worms, *Enchytraeus*, are a highly recommended food for discus. Photo by Bernd Degen.

Tubifex, long a staple food for discus, is not recommended for the tank-raised discus. They are sewer worms and should NOT be handled without gloves. Photo by Mark Smith.

Vinegar eels are excellent food for baby discus. Photo by MP&C Piednoir.

FEEDING DISCUS

The Blue-red Turquoise developed by Gan Aquarium Fish Farm in Singapore. Photo by K.H. Chew.

the parasite *Oodinium*, which is able to wipe out an entire spawn of young discus within forty-eight hours if undetected. Live adult brine, however, are a safe food and can be purchased in most good aquarium shops.

The second live food that is an excellent choice for the discus is the white worm, *Enchytraeus*.

This terrestrial worm harbors no damaging parasites. White worms are very popular as discus food with European breeders and can be propagated easily in temperatures of 60 - 65 degrees Fahrenheit. It has been said that white worms are too fatty as a discus food unless they are fed very sparingly, but they can be fed to your fish on a daily basis if the food for the worms has a low fat content. It is generally too warm in southern Florida for me to successfully raise white worms, but I have had success during our winter months feeding the worms nothing but plain low-fat yogurt.

Garden earthworms are an excellent live food for discus, although they are not always available. They are generally a safe discus food. Several years ago we found what we thought would be a good source for earthworms, one of the many fishing bait shops in South Florida where the worms are sold to bass fishermen who fish the Florida Everglades. The earthworms are available in different sizes, so we naturally bought the smallest ones available. Was this a perfect live food? No! After feeding the worms we found our discus turning dark in color and emphatically in

Brine shrimp is the ideal food for discus and most other aquarium fishes. This is a magnified view of adult brine shrimp which grow to about half an inch. Photo courtesy of San Francisco Bay Brand.

FEEDING DISCUS

distress. Why? We found that the worms, which are raised commercially on worm farms, must be sprayed with a repellent in order to keep mites out of the cultures. As soon as we stopped feeding the earthworms, conditions returned to normal. On the other hand, if you have access to clean worms, perhaps from your own garden, you should attempt to include them in your discus feeding program.

Once they have become accustomed to their surroundings and the coming and going of their keeper, discus often will accept food from the hand.

Only high quality flake foods for discus contain the highest concentration of carotenoid pigments to bring out the colors in discus and other tropical fish. Photo courtesy of O.S.I. Marine Lab, Inc.

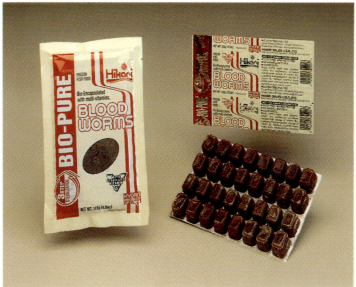

Bloodworms are an excellent food source for your discus, and they are available frozen for guaranteed freshness. Photo courtesy of Hikari.

PREPARED FOODS

Two other forms of discus food available to the hobbyist today are dry and frozen foods. I will attempt to be impartial in my evaluation of the dry foods for discus, as several of my discus formulas, as well as my formulas for other tropical fishes, are sold worldwide in frozen form.

There has been much improvement over the past several years in the quality of flake and pellet foods for freshwater tropical fishes. These vitamin-enriched foods certainly do have a place in a feeding program for discus, although I feel that they should be looked upon as supplementary foods to be fed perhaps once daily instead of being considered the main discus diet.

We attempt to feed our frozen discus formulas to all our young fish as soon as we remove them from their parents or, when raising them apart from their parents, until we remove them from the pans. In many cases we do, at that time, feed them newly-hatched brine shrimp. But with the potential danger of *Oodinimum* when feeding baby *Artemia*, we try to circumvent the brine shrimp and proceed directly to our frozen discus fry formula.

Once the young discus have eagerly accepted our frozen fry formula, we continue to feed them the same food until they reach the point in their growth at which they are able to eat our frozen discus formula for adult fish. Discus breeders have asked us why we feed only one food to our fish when it is common knowledge that discus, as well as all other tropicals, should have a varied diet. I ask them to look at the label on our package to see the list of ingredients that we include. The "single food" that we use is, in reality, a complete and balanced diet consisting of heart, krill, shrimp, clam, liver, spinach, wheat germ, and *Spirulina*, plus all essential vitamins and minerals.

The protein content of the food is 50%, and all the ingredients are raw, with the exception of the liver, which is lightly parboiled. One might

Young discus attacking frozen bloodworms as they fall loosely though the water. Photo by Bernd Degen.

question why we have added both spinach and *Spirulina* to the formula when it is known that discus are carnivorous. The truth is that discus, in reality, are omnivorous, and require green food in their diet. The green food acts as a mild laxative, thus keeping the delicate intestinal tract clear. Our hatchery is not well lighted, so there is never any resulting algal growth, but I have seen many well lighted discus tanks with a lush growth of green algae and the discus subsequently feeding off the algae.

Two other foods that we are presently feeding our discus are garlic and bananas. Needless to say, the garlic can be mixed into any discus formula, which is what we do in our hatchery. There are no problems regarding the acceptance of the garlic by the discus. What made us think of adding garlic to the food? Garlic acts as a deterrent against the proliferation of intestinal worms in discus. It will not kill the worms outright, but if fed on a regular basis to discus harboring intestinal worms, the garlic will, over time, stop the recurring reproductive cycle of the worms.

Bananas! Why bananas for discus? We conducted an experiment several years ago in a number of control tanks to determine the growth rate of young discus by feeding them different foods. We were able to maintain the same growth rate on the discus in the tank where the fish were fed only bananas as in all the other control tanks, but only for a period of three weeks. After that time the banana-fed discus began to fall back in

Good feeding means the discus grow at the same size. If there are runts, they should be removed and raised separately. Photo by Bernd Degen.

growth. The experiment convinced me, however, that bananas most certainly could be used as a nourishing additive in any discus food formula.

It is important to discuss the frequency of feeding discus. We can get the most rapid growth in our young fish by feeding them a minimum of three times daily. If you are one of the many who believe it best to feed young discus nine or ten times per day, that is fine, as long as you keep pollution levels under control by using an extremely efficient filtration system or by making frequent water changes. Another point to consider regarding numerous daily feedings is that your discus must have ample time to digest their food before the next feeding is made. It is important that all food from the previous feeding has been consumed before the next

feeding. If you attempt to rush the discus the result will almost certainly be a tank of sick and constipated fish.

When our discus reach sexual maturity we cut back to one feeding per day. With few exceptions, for this once-a-day feeding we use our formulated frozen discus diet. Nevertheless, on occasion they are fed either live or frozen *Artemia*. Other foods that adult discus accept are bloodworms, *Daphnia*, and mosquito larvae, which are generally obtainable in freeze-dried and frozen form.

One problem that many discus hobbyists share is that they often have a difficult time getting their adult discus to accept a new food. Under most circumstances, young discus have an easy time accepting a new food. Adult discus are creatures of habit, however, and the introduction of a new food can be some-

The Green Discus, *Symphysodon a. aequifasciata*, tending her brood. When the baby fish become hungry they eat the slime covering the parents' bodies. Photo by Hans J. Mayland.

FEEDING DISCUS

Discus are happy and content if they take foods from your hand. Photo by Bernd Degen.

what unsettling to them. With a bit of patience your discus can be induced to accept the new food very easily. Simply mix about 10% of the new food into their regular food on the first day. They may accept the food inadvertently, or more likely, they may completely refuse it. By the third or fourth day they will be familiar enough with the new food that there will be at least some acceptance. At this point increase the new food to approximately 25%, and if it is accepted, you can then make daily withdrawals of the original food so that by the end of a ten-day period your discus are eagerly accepting the new food undiluted.

The critical period to achieve maximum growth on your young discus is in their first 28 weeks. If they are shortchanged during this period regarding water quality and frequency of water changes they will never attain their optimum size. Water with a high mineral content is critical for their maximum growth, as discus require the iron, calcium, magnesium, and other essential vitamins and minerals for proper bone structure and tissue growth. An excellent discus breeder in Ft. Lauderdale, Florida grows out his young fish in water from a 65- foot-deep well with a conductivity of 700 ppm and a pH of 7.5. It would be difficult to surpass the growth rate that he has attained by using this water. Most hobbyists, however, do not have access to well water and must rely on municipal water, reverse osmosis, or deionized water.

This is an Alancer Red discus with a scale anomaly. This variety was never popular and has disappeared from the marketplace. Photo by K.H. Chew courtesy of Gan Aquarium Fish.

Purchasing Discus

Obviously the first place that comes to mind when you're looking to buy young discus is the pet shop or tropical fish specialty store. But in many cases you might not like the way your pet shop's discus look. In such cases you might have to buy your discus from a breeder.

How many discus should one purchase at a time? Purchasing only two discus for the tank will more than likely be a mistake even if both fish are the same size. The reason is that sooner or later— usually sooner— one of the two fish will exert its power in the aquarium and totally dominate the second fish. In doing so, it will not allow its tankmate to feed or swim freely without being chased or harassed. If this persists for any extended period of time, the second fish will cease to grow normally and in some cases will eventually die. For this reason it is best to initially purchase at least four or five discus, in which case the dominant one won't be able to take its aggression out on a single fish, and with four or five tankmates there will be enough movement and confusion at feeding time to give all of them a chance. But why not simply remove the dominant fish in the first place so that the fish can settle down? In a group of four or five discus, the second most dominant fish would then take over. This is, of course, nothing more than the natu-

A six-week old baby discus showing excellent roundness of the body. Photo by Bernd Degen.

ral pecking order in nature establishing itself.

For the novice discus hobbyist, it is wise to have some basic knowledge of freshwater fishkeeping before making the initial discus purchase. With that in hand, probably the best size fish to purchase would be approximately two inches, for several reasons. At that size they adjust quickly to their new surroundings, much more so than larger discus do, and they do not suffer the trauma or stress in the move from the dealer's tank to the hobbyist's tank. All this is critical if your discus have been bought from an out-of-state dealer and have been shipped to you by air freight. We fully expect the young discus that we ship via air freight to be eating in the hobbyist's tank on the same day that the fish are shipped.

If the hobbyist is in a position to personally select his discus from the dealer's tank there are several guidelines he must follow. First, if the hobbyist selects the largest fish in the tank, will he end up with all males? No, not necessarily. At the two-inch size it is too early for the males to have begun to develop into a larger size than the females, so I would definitely choose the largest, most robust fish in the tank. Make certain that the dealer has not just fed the discus in that

Healthy young discus show an eager curiosity when they are attracted by food even in the crowded temporary conditions of the wholesaler. Photo by Bernd Degen.

particular tank, because transferring any discus from one tank to another on a full stomach will probably result in their getting sick, most likely from a bloating condition caused by stress.

The size of the eyes, in relation to the overall size of the fish, should give a clear indication of whether or not the fish have been given the proper care during the crucial grow-out period. The eyes should be red or orange in color and small in size. Eye coloring that is dark gray or black, or eyes that are abnormally large, indicate poor care or an existing disease.

In the home aquarium, your discus should be up to the front glass in the tank and actively looking for food when you enter the room. In the dealer's tank, the young discus should be active and moving about the tank with authority. If any are dark in color or huddled in a back corner of the tank, they are probably sick. Such discus, of course, are to be avoided.

Many young discus manifest visible fin or gill deformities, nearly always attributed to either a genetic problem or a water problem. A fin deformity will usually show up as a malformed anal fin. There are times, however, when the fin deformity is caused by a bacterial problem in the water at the time that the fry are very small and delicate. I have seen, on occasion, tanks of tiny discus with what resembled a true bacterial bloom in the water, in which case the fry were destined to have deformed fins. When the gills on the fish are not properly formed, poor water quality or a genetic imbalance is generally the cause. When either of these deformities is caused by poor water quality, the young fish can still be used as future breeders, as the gill and fin problems will not be passed on to the next generation. On the other hand, most of us do not want to raise young deformed fish in hopes of being able to eventually breed them.

PURCHASING DISCUS

While this discus is well colored, it has an undesirable shape. It is not rounded enough. Photo by Arend van den Nieuwenhuizen.

The eggs of a discus, having been laid on an Amazon swordplant, are tended by the mother fish. The father fish is just below. Photo by Arend van den Nieuwenhuizen.

Breeding

In their wild habitat, discus breed during the rainy season when the Amazonian streams overflow and result in an overabundance of food. In the home aquarium, however, discus can be bred at any time of the year. Are discus easy to breed? Yes, as long as they are healthy and free of parasites.

The hobbyist's ultimate achievement with discus is generally considered to be a pair that successfully raise a spawn of their own. Many hobbyists contact us to ask if we sell mated pairs of our discus, and needless to say, they are informed that we need all of our discus pairs for ourselves. The best advice I can give concerning breeding is to forget about any instant gratification and instead obtain a number of young fish and allow them to pair off naturally upon reaching sexual maturity. If the hobbyist is in a position to obtain a number of sexually mature discus, how does he determine the sex of each fish? In

A Hong Kong specialty is the deep blue color, the elongated dorsal fin and the very deep form. The cobalt blue color of this fish is very attractive. Photo by Fumitoshi Mori.

most cases this is difficult to establish. Over the years we have found that adult discus from the same spawn can, on most occasions, be sexed properly. The males will generally be more colorful and larger and will have a more highly developed dorsal fin. Interestingly, however, on a recent visit to Hong Kong, a local discus breeder showed me one of his new discus strains in which the females, when fully developed, were larger than the males.

Let us assume that you have six to eight sexually mature discus in a 70-gallon tank and that one morning you notice that two of them have taken over a corner of the tank, driving the remaining fish to the other end of the tank. You now have your first pair of discus! It is not absolutely necessary to have an object in the tank on which

This female laid her eggs on the intake side of a foam filter! Photo by Bernd Degen.

When discus develop a taste for their own eggs, a screen is placed over the eggs so the parents can't eat them. The screen does not discourage the parents from fanning the eggs and protecting the young.

the fish can spawn. In Malaysia most of the commercial discus breeders have nothing in their tanks for the discus to spawn on, so the pairs spawn on the glass.

In our tanks, discus pairs generally spawn on the PVC drain tubes. Most of our pairs take excellent care of their spawns, but occasionally we have pairs that are inveterate egg-eaters. In those instances, we install a PVC sleeve that fits over the drain tube, and when the spawning is complete we remove the PVC sleeve and hatch the spawn artificially. Removing the spawn from the parents obviously prevents the parents from caring for the eggs during the hatching period and further prevents the babies from feeding off their parents' skin secretions, which necessitates that they be fed artificially, but it's a method that we use for a sizable percentage of all of our spawnings. We're going to cover my method of artificial rearing of discus fry, but we'll cover the natural way first.

Symphysodon discus discus fighting over territory prior to spawning. These battles rarely cause damage. Photo by Arend van den Nieuwenhuizen.

NATURAL HATCHING TECHNIQUE

After the eggs have been laid, the pair will fan and "mouth" them, keeping them clean and free of any debris that might be in the tank. Unfortunately, some discus parents are worse than just neglectful in this regard. Instead of protecting and caring for the eggs, they eat them. There are times when only one of the parents is an egg-eater, in which case the culprit can be removed and the spawn left with the remaining parent. One adult spawning discus, male or female, can competently resume care of the spawn.

What should be done differently now that the hobbyist has achieved his first discus spawn? Nothing at all! Many hobbyists tell me that when they see their first successful discus spawn they want to darken the tank or perhaps cover the sides of the tank. They ask if they should discontinue making regular water changes. I stress that nothing should be changed regarding routine care.

The eggs generally hatch within sixty to seventy hours, depending on the water temperature. The warmer the tank water is, the less time will be required for hatching. In our hatchery, an average spawn will consist of approximately 150 to 170 fry. As the fry develop and become stronger, they will begin to free themselves from the receptacle where they were laid and dart about the tank in a disorganized manner. Do not panic when this happens! Little by little, as the fry become free swimming they will locate their parents' sides and begin to feed.

The fry generally feed from one parent at a time, with the feeding period lasting about two to three minutes, after which time the feeding parent

This pair laid their eggs on the glass. The glass side of the aquarium is actually a mirror that's the cause of the confusing image.

BREEDING

A discus of very mixed parentage cleaning off the spawning cone preparatory to depositing her eggs. Photo by Bernd Degen.

will brush the fry off with a quick move toward the other parent. We use a dim 10-watt night light during night hours when we have young discus fry feeding from their parents. In this way the fry can continue to eat during the night with no interruption.

Under normal conditions, the feeding fry should have doubled in size after approximately thirty hours; and after having fed from the parents' sides for six to seven days they should be ready for their introduction to newly-hatched *Artemia* (brine shrimp). The brine shrimp are siphoned into a fine mesh net and rinsed in fresh water while still in the net, then gently placed over the fry. Will the fry accept the brine shrimp? Probably not the first time, but they will familiarize themselves with it, and by the second or third feeding they will venture farther away from the parents and eagerly consume the shrimp.

During the period that the fry are eating the newly hatched brine shrimp, they will continue to eat from their parents' bodies. We normally leave the fry with their parents until we are assured that all are consuming the shrimp and are able to become independent of the parents.

When ready for the transfer from their parents, and with a simple sponge filter already installed in a 10-gallon tank, the young can be caught in a soft net and transferred to the new tank, or they can be

The immense pleasure of watching discus care for their fry in a normal manner more than compensates for the occasional lost spawn eaten by the parents. Here the three-week-old fry have switched from feeding on the father to feeding on the mother. Photo by Bernd Degen.

BREEDING

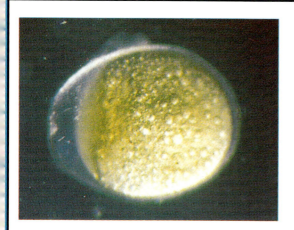
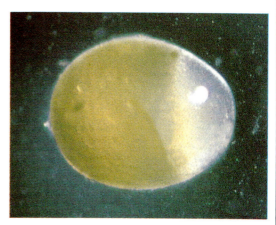

This wonderful series of photos shows a typical discus egg during its 64 hour development process from being fertilized to hatching out. Photos by Horst Linke.

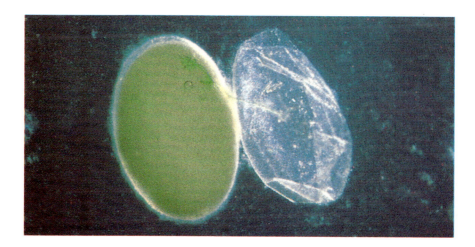

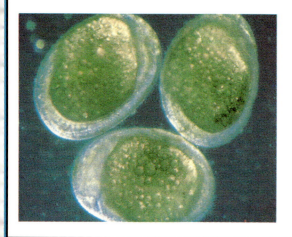

The lumps on the head of this newly hatched discus fry are adhesive glands by which the baby adheres to a surface. Discus usually stick to a spot as they develop. Photo by Horst Linke.

As the baby discus matures, it lives from the yolk in the yolk sac. This baby's sac is half empty and it must soon start searching for food. Discus babies do not search for food until they are free-swimming. Photo by Horst Linke.

BREEDING

siphoned out directly into the new tank. In the new tank it is best to use the water from the parents' tank, where the water hardness and pH will be the same.

At this point your young discus are on their own and are no longer dependent on their parents. The fry should be fed the newly-hatched brine shrimp at least three times a day, with the hobbyist ascertaining that all food has been consumed before attempting to feed again. It is essential that the tank be kept clean at all times. At this point it is important to make daily water changes of approximately 30% each time. In doing so your discus will avoid the digestive problems that can occur with heavy feedings and infrequent water changes. I recommend maintaining a water temperature of 86 degrees Fahrenheit during this initial period, tapering off to approximately 82 - 84 degrees Fahrenheit after six weeks.

ARTIFICIAL HATCHING TECHNIQUE

The artificial hatching system requires that the eggs be removed from the parents and hatched in a separate aquarium. Alternatively, you could remove the parents from the spawning tank and leave the eggs in it, but then you'd be hatching the eggs in far larger quarters than they require; in effect, you'd be wasting that tank space. Additionally, the newly hatched fry would tend to get lost in a big tank. In our hatchery we use rectangular all-glass tanks of one gallon capacity to hold the egg-bearing site after it has been removed from the spawning tank. The spawning site usually will be a piece of slate or a breeding cone or even a leaf, wherever the eggs were laid. In our hatchery the eggs are routinely laid on removable PVC sleeves that cover outlet drains in the spawning tanks, but they can be laid just about anywhere, with the sides of the tank occasionally being chosen. In such cases the eggs can be removed to the hatching tank, but it's a

Newly hatched fry in the hatching tank. The author uses more methylene blue. Photo by Y. Kong.

After the period of eating the slime from their parents, the fry look for other foods and this is the time to offer them newly hatched brine shrimp, *Artemia*. Photo by Arend van den Nieuwenhuizen.

delicate operation. They have to be *carefully* peeled off the glass directly into a net and placed into the hatching unit. We use single-edged razor blades for the peeling operation, and we make sure that they're very thoroughly washed and wiped before use to make sure that any oil or other foreign matter on them is removed.

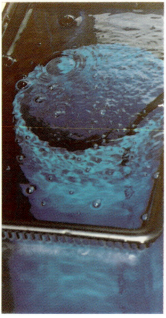

The author's egg-bearing sleeve in a hatching tank. Photo by Dr. Herbert R. Axelrod.

The water in the hatching unit is treated with fourteen drops of a 1% solution of methylene blue as a fungus preventive, and it is a weak bactericide as well. The hatching water, incidentally, is not the same water as is used in the tanks housing adult discus. It's from a separate stock of water that we keep in a 300-gallon holding tank. It's from our local water supply, but it has been treated to remove chloramines; it also has been treated with peat and has a pH of 6.2-6.4 and a hardness reading of 250 microsiemens. The water in the adult discus tanks is reverse osmosis water that is softer (75 microsiemens).

The water in the hatching units generally is maintained at a temperature of between 82 and 84 F, because that's the ambient temperature in the hatchery. The temperature in the hatchery often goes to over 90 F during the summer and occasionally

The sleeve, removed from the hatching tank for photographic purposes, indicates how the eggs have been dyed blue by the methylene blue, yet they are still alive and hatched well. Photo by Dr. Herbert R. Axelrod.

during those periods in the winter when it's cold enough outside to make heating the hatchery necessary, because the hatching area is very near the heater. The abnormally high temperatures don't seem to have a bad effect on the eggs or fry. It might even do them some good, but I don't think it would be wise to keep the temperature that high for protracted periods.

The eggs, by the way, are not kept in the methylene blue-treated water for the entire time before they hatch. They (and the site to which they're attached, of course) are taken out and placed in unmedicated clean water in the pan in which they'll finally hatch and be fed. This is done about 52 hours after the eggs have been put into the initial hatching unit. One very practical reason for moving the unhatched eggs and putting them into the feeding pan is that it's a lot easier to move the eggladen breeding site than it is to remove the individual hatched fry. While the eggs are still in the hatching unit a weak flow of air is directed over the surface of the water ; too strong a stream of bubbles would be harmful.

The feeding pans themselves don't have to be very big. The ones used in our hatchery are circular, a little less than a foot wide (eleven inches by actual measurement) and three inches deep, so they hold only about a gallon and a quarter when filled to the top. The pans are metal, but their insides are enameled in white; we get them from a hospital supply house. The white enamel surface of the inside of the pans makes it easier to see the fry once they hatch, since the fry contrast against the white of the pan. Glass pans or bowls could be used also, but the fry would be harder to see in them.

The fry hatch out after the eggs have been in the pan for about six hours, and they stay attached to the spawning site for a while longer. They start to drop off onto the bottom of the pan in about a day to a day and half after having hatched. Once all of the fry are off the spawning site—we sometimes have to coax some of them off by directing a gentle stream of water over them from a narrow-mouthed surgical syringe—the spawning site can be removed from the pan. The fry will stay congregated in clumps at the bottom of the pan for about two days; they'll then begin to disengage from their clumps and begin individually scooting around the bottom of the pan for a few hours. Finally they'll begin to move up to the top of the feeding pan. They shouldn't be fed until most of the fry have reached or nearly reached the surface. Definitely *don't* feed them while all or most are at the bottom of the pan. We treat the water in the full pan with twenty milligrams of Furan-2, a powder in capsule form; we usually use it in the form of a stock solution to add to the pan water.

During the time the eggs and later the fry are in the feeding pan, regular partial water changes must continue to be made. Two changes a day, with each change being about forty percent, would be fine. The changes should be made gently, without disturbing the water too much. Gentle aeration is provided during all of this time also. No airstone is used, but an open airline tube is allowed to play a very slow stream over the top of the water.

The author uses these feeding pans which are 11 inches in diameter and 3 inches deep with VERY mild aeration. Photo by Dr. Herbert R. Axelrod.

Artificial Food Formula

My formula is based mostly on egg yolk fortified with *Spirulina* powder and crushed newly hatched brine shrimp. The egg yolk must be supplied in equal proportions from raw yolk and hard-boiled yolk. Both the raw egg alone and the hard-boiled yolk alone wouldn't have the proper pasty consistency to adhere to the sides of the feeding pan; they have to be mixed in order to get the food to stick. The two types of yolk must be mixed together thoroughly, which turns them into a gluey paste. To the paste is added just enough *Spirulina* powder to turn the entire mixture a light yellow-green. If too much of the green powder is added, the mixture will lose its stickiness. The entire preparation is then formed into a flat patty before it's placed into a plastic bag and frozen.

The next step is to add live baby brine shrimp to the egg yolk/*Spirulina* mixture. Obviously that requires that you have live baby brine shrimp on hand, so you'll have had to have set up a hatching culture somewhere along the line. After thawing out the egg yolk/*Spirulina* mixture on a paper towel, mix the brine shrimp (rinse them first) after first removing as much water as possible by placing them onto a paper towel. Use a proportion of about four parts egg yolk/*Spirulina* to about one part brine shrimp. You can do the mixing right in the palm of your hand after first making sure that your hands have been thoroughly rinsed after being washed; you certainly don't want any soap residue mixed into the food. As with the addition of *Spirulina* to the mixture, adding too much

Artemia also will have a bad effect on its adherence to the pan.

You can get away without mixing the baby brine shrimp into the concoction, but the fry will do better with it. In fact, they'll do better with it than they'll do with their parents' skin secretions. The fry should be fed on the formula for three full days before graduating to their next food.

Applying the formula is a relatively tricky operation, but here's the best way to go about it. First siphon the feeding pan about halfway down, then thoroughly dry off the upper half of the pan with a clean and dry paper towel. With the formula in the palm of your hand, use a finger of the other hand to apply a very thin bead in a narrow (say about three-eighths of an inch wide) band to the entire perimeter of the inside of the pan. Then give the band of formula about a quarter of an hour to dry before you raise the water level in the feeding pan enough to cover the formula. If the band doesn't dry properly, or the formula hasn't been put onto the pan correctly, the band will slough off into the water and you'll have to start the operation all over again. If your hatching room is very humid it might take longer than a quarter of an hour for the formula to dry, but you don't want to let it dry out for too long in any event, because then the formula will get too hard for the fry to graze from even after it gets soaked when the water level is raised.

Keep in mind that it is going to be as important to make partial water changes in the feeding pan as it is to make them in the regular tanks. In fact, they're going to be even more important to make in the feeding pan, partly because there is so little water in the pan and partly because the feeding formula, with all of that egg yolk in it and at the temperature (82 to 86 F) that the feeding pan should be maintained at, is highly subject to decay. In our hatchery we like to make the babies' first feeding at about 7:30 in the morning, then change the water at about 1:00 in the afternoon, with another change at about 7:00 in the evening and another at about 1:00 AM. The bigger the feeding pan, the less frequent the changes. When making the water changes we siphon out as much water as we can without leaving the babies high and dry.

We make the last feeding at about 7:00 PM, and about four hours after that we take all of the food out of the pan; we drain the pan to near the bottom, making sure that the babies have just enough water to swim in and not much more, at the same time siphoning out uneaten food from the bottom and then swabbing the inside of the pan with a clean paper towel to remove the food on the sides.

The second and third days of feeding with the artificial formula should proceed the same way as the first. During this period you should remove any defective fry that develop. After the third day of feeding with the formula, you can move on to feeding the fry with live baby brine shrimp. You can tell whether the fry are accepting the baby brine shrimp by checking their color. If they're eating the shrimp they—or at least their bellies—will become pinkish to orange, as opposed to the gray color they have while they're feeding on the for-

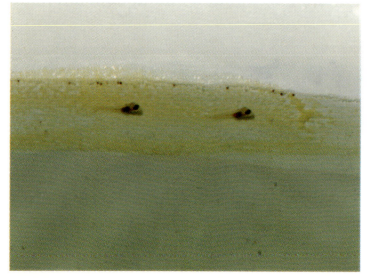

Young fish, 5 days old, eating the formula which has been smeared along the upper edge of the feeding pan. Photo by Dr. Herbert R. Axelrod.

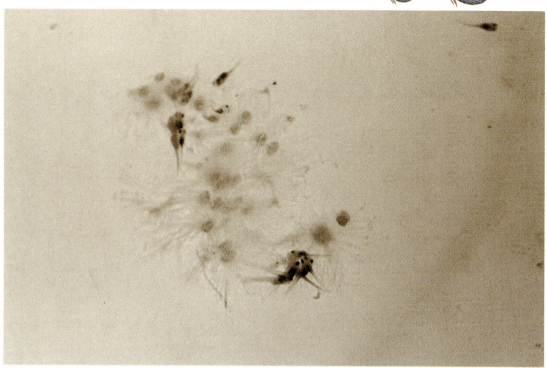

Eggs left without their parents often die and become fungused. This fungus can spread to healthy eggs which are adjacent. This photos shows the fungused eggs and the healthy fry 78 hours after being laid.

mula. After the third day on the formula most of the fry should accept the shrimp, but those that don't can be left on the formula for another day. For the first three days or so of feeding with the baby brine shrimp, lower the water level in the pan to between an inch and an inch and a quarter, because the shrimp will be congregating at the bottom of the pan. You have to strike a balance between too few and too many *Artemia* in the pan; too few and the fry won't have enough to eat, too many and you have a big mess.

When you make the regular afternoon water change, remove almost all of the old water and as much of the uneaten brine shrimp as you can. When you make the nighttime water change, remove as much of the brine shrimp as are left in the pan, plus all the fish waste and any other organic matter, then fill the pan to the top. Let it stay that way until the next morning, when you again lower the level and feed with baby brine shrimp. Beginning with the third day of *Artemia* feeding, you can slowly raise the level of the water until in about two or three days it's at the top of the pan, because by that time the fry will have become more aggressive in chasing down the brine shrimp and will pursue them all over the pan.

After three or four more days on the brine feedings the fry will be ready to be transferred to bigger—but still not too big, say only two gallons—tanks; keep up the gentle aeration in these tanks. The size of the spawn will determine how long the fry stay in their new quarters. The larger the spawn, the shorter the time they'll be there. With us, spawns of more than one hundred fry are kept in the 2-gallon tanks for no more than seven days. Then they're moved into 20-gallon tanks or even larger tanks. Be careful when moving the fry into larger quarters that you don't subject them to an abrupt increase in the amount of water turbulence from aeration and filtration. After the fry are in the larger tanks they are introduced to the Jack Wattley Discus Fry Food that is available in frozen form; they should be introduced to it, and to any other new food for that matter, gradually, a little bit at a time.

Diseases

Discusfishes are not at all disease-prone. Nevertheless, as with all other living organisms, there are times when an individual fish, or perhaps a number of your discus, will be sick. If your total discus-care program, consisting of a proper feeding routine, water quality and water changes, etc., is in order, you will be practicing "preventive action." Prevent the problem before it becomes a problem!

When discus breeders have sufficient fish from different bloodlines, it is not necessary to go "outside" to continue a healthy breeding program. At times, however, it is necessary to introduce fish from other breeding stock into the hatchery. These fish, regardless of how healthy they appear, are placed in quarantine tanks in a quarantined room. How long should these new infusions be maintained in their quarantine tanks? In our hatchery we generally keep them there for a period of four to six weeks.

There is a plethora of tropical fish books available for the discus hobbyist describing in detail the diseases to which discus are vulnerable. Because of space limitations only a few of the more common diseases will be discussed here.

Bacterial infections in discus, as well as in other tropical fishes, are probably the number one culprit. If the hobbyist finds tiny pinhead craters over the eyes and around the bony cartilage area of the head, or a degeneration of the discus fins or tail, he can strongly suspect that the problem is one of *Pseudomonas* or *Aeromonas* bacteria. The bacteria, if the infection is bacterial in origin, will be either gram positive or gram negative. The average hobbyist will not have the capability to determine which type of bacteria is causing the problem, and for that reason will have to resort to a broad-spectrum antibiotic that covers most (but not all) gram-positive and gram-negative bacteria. These antibiotics are readily available in aquarium shops.

Another method of treating bacterial infections is by lowering the pH of the tank water. In many cases I prefer this method, as it does not require any medication. To successfully achieve this, the water must be soft. The pH, starting for example at 6.5, can usually be lowered to 6.0

This discus is developing an infected area over the head above and between the eyes plus on the caudal peduncle (base of the tail). It is either a *Pseudomonas* or *Aeromonas* infection.

DISEASES

An 8 week old discus showing a short gill cover. Fish like these should not be used for breeding. Photo by Bernd Degen.

with no problem. Wait approximately eight hours before further lowering the pH to 5.5. At this point it is best to wait another twenty-four hours before lowering the pH to 5.0. By now you will probably have arrested the bacterial growth on the fish to a great extent, but it is wise to continue the treatment until the pH has been lowered to 4.5. It is important to watch closely for any signs of stress in the fish; if there are none the hobbyist can, after another eight-hour wait, make the final pH drop, this time to 4.0. During the pH treatment it is necessary to continue to make normal water changes. Maintain the 4.0 pH for a week, after which you can make the gradual pH rise to your normal 6.5 or so. Take several days to effect this change.

Parasitical gill flukes can cause much harm to young discus. Without a microscope, how does the hobbyist know whether his discus have flukes? Under normal conditions the respiration rate of discus is approximately 60 to 70 breaths per minute. If your fish are breathing more than 90 times a minute, you can be fairly certain that the problem is one of gill flukes, either the live-bearing *Gyrodactylus* or the more common egg-laying *Dactylogyrus*. For both of these fluke species there are excellent remedies available in aquarium shops.

Intestinal parasites are generally in the form of the worm *Capillaria* or the more common flagellate *Hexamita*. Both *Capillaria*, which is a nematode, and *Hexamita* can be found in many discus. Under optimum conditions (which seldom exist) these internal parasites are not necessarily debilitating, but if tank conditions are not the best, they can cause much damage to discus. *Hexamita* can be found in discus that have generally stopped eating. The fish usually show long, stringlike gray feces. A heavy infestation of *Hexamita* will cause discus to lose weight rapidly, but with an increase in the aquarium water temperature to 92 degrees Fahrenheit for a week, along with the proper dosage of Flagyl (Metronidazole), the *Hexamita* infestation will be controlled, and the fish will very quickly regain any lost weight. The hobbyist will find Flagyl readily available in aquarium shops.

The drug of choice to treat *Capillaria*, as well as tapeworms, has been Flubendazole. Over the past several years, we have heard a number of comments that perhaps the drug, in controlling the worms, can have serious and harmful after-treatment effects. We have made extensive controlled

This is a VERY sick discus. It is also starving. It shows symptoms of many diseases. Photo by Bernd Degen.

These discus are almost perfectly healthy. The front fish shows a wound with missing scales. This later became infected and was finally attacked by fungus and the fish died. This color variety is the cobalt-turquoise and was bred and photographed by Dr. Clifford Chan in Singapore

tests in our hatchery using fresh garlic for the control of all internal worms in discus. These tests, over the past eight years, have been conducted in Ft. Lauderdale as well as in Rockford, Illinois. We have had excellent results and are pleased to have been able to control the *Capillaria*, as well as other worms, by using a natural homeopathic approach rather than by having to administer a drug.

To achieve optimum results using this treatment, the hobbyist must administer freshly squeezed garlic liquid onto the discus food of his choice. This is not a quick-fix type of treatment. The garlic should be added to the food at each feeding to achieve maximum results. As garlic is a healthful food for humans, we use the liquid on a daily basis for all our discus even though they do not harbor internal worms. The amount of garlic added to the food should be approximately two cubic centimeters for eight ounces of food. Garlic oil in capsule form can be obtained in a natural foods store, but to obtain the best results the garlic must be freshly squeezed. Unfortunately, if the discus with intestinal worms are not eating, it will be necessary to resort to using Flubendazole.